This Couple's Date Adventure Journal belongs to:

_____ & _____

Together since:

_____

Date Icon Guide

 Dates that involve food or drink

 Dates that involve conversation

 Dates that you can do from home

 Dates that involve learning

 Dates that must be completed outdoors

 Dates that may require a flight

 Dates that require good weather

 Dates that may require a road trip

 Dates that are for lazy days

 Dates that require an overnight stay

 Dates that are romantic/intimate

 Dates that are affordable

 Dates that involve creativity

 Dates that are moderately priced

 Double Dates!

 Dates that are more pricey or expensive

 Dates that involve exercise

 Date conditions are decided by YOU

Date Categories

Can You Feel The Love?

Romantic dates to help
you re-ignite the flame

Date Idea #1:
Pretend You're Strangers

Arrange to meet up at a public area of your choosing and pretend you're meeting for the first time. See where it goes!

Place Photo Here

Date complete: _____

Favorite memories:

_____

_____

_____

_____

_____

Date Idea #2:
Re-create Your First Date

❷

Try to recreate every detail from start to finish.
Bring that first-date butterflies feeling back again!

Place Photo Here

Date complete: _____

Favorite memories:

_____

_____

_____

_____

_____

Date Idea #3:
Drive-In Movie and Picnic

Enjoy a picnic in your car (or on its hood) while you watch a drive-in movie of your choice.

Date complete: _____

Favorite memories:

_____

_____

_____

_____

_____

Date Idea #4:
Star Gazing

Find a quiet place where you can see them shine. Lay down next to each other and look up in silence.

Place Photo Here

Date complete: _____

Favorite memories:

_____

_____

_____

_____

_____

Date Idea #5:
DIY Home Spa

Take turns massaging and pampering one another. Think dim lights, relaxing music, body oils, candlelight, etc...

Date complete: _____

Favorite memories:

_____

_____

_____

_____

_____

Date Idea #6:
Fancy Restaurant

Go to a fancy restaurant in your area and splurge on some high-end entrees and desserts.

Date complete: _____

Favorite memories:

_____

_____

_____

_____

_____

Date Idea #7:
Dine in The Dark At Home

🏠 🍴 🗣️ 🌿 💲

Wait until it's dark out, and set up dinner for two. With all the lights closed, eat and chat in complete darkness.

Place Photo Here

Date complete: _____

Favorite memories:

_____

_____

_____

_____

_____

Date Idea #8:
Paddleboat and Talk

Rent a paddleboat and paddle your way out to a quiet area.
Have a deep conversation about whatever you'd like.

Place Photo Here

Date complete: _____

Favorite memories:

_____

_____

_____

_____

_____

Date Idea #9:
Slow Dance in the Rain

On a rainy day, spontaneously grab your partner and go outside. Play your favorite songs on your phone and dance.

Place Photo Here

Date complete: _____

Favorite memories:

_____

_____

_____

_____

_____

Date Idea #10:
Sunrise and Sunset

Watch the sunrise and sunset together on the same day.
Find a good place to watch both.

Place Photo Here

Date complete: _____

Favorite memories:

_____

_____

_____

_____

_____

Easy and
Stress Free

Dates for lazy days to help
you relax and stay connected

Date Idea #11
Shhh...It's A Library

Visit your local library and pick out some good reads. Find a place to sit and enjoy some quiet reading time together.

Date complete: _____

Favorite memories:

_____

_____

_____

_____

_____

Date Idea #12:
Childhood Movie Marathon

Spend a day watching all of your favorite nostalgic childhood movies and eating all of your favorite snacks.

Place Photo Here

Date complete: _____

Favorite memories:

_____

_____

_____

_____

_____

Date Idea #13:
Build a fort

Build a fort in your home using supplies you find around the house. Then enjoy some cuddle time and good conversation.

Place Photo Here

Date complete: _____

Favorite memories:

_____

_____

_____

_____

_____

Date Idea #14:
Stay in Bed All Day!

🏠🍃🐕🗣️

The only exceptions are to take bathroom breaks and to get food. Spend time watching movies, talking, or other stuff...

Place Photo Here

Date complete: _____

Favorite memories:

_____

_____

_____

_____

_____

Date Idea #15:
Couples Spa Day

Go to a couple's spa, and enjoy a day of relaxing music, couples massages, facials, and quiet together time.

Place Photo Here

Date complete: _____

Favorite memories:

_____

_____

_____

_____

_____

Date Idea #16:
Talking Games

Play talking games like would you rather, truth or dare, or never have I ever, and learn something new about each other.

Place Photo Here

Date complete: _____

Favorite memories:

_____

_____

_____

_____

_____

Date Idea #17:
Visit an Animal Cafe

Have a cup of coffee and enjoy the experience of being surrounded by furry friends as you eat and drink.

Place Photo Here

Date complete: _____

Favorite memories:

_____

_____

_____

_____

_____

Date Idea #18:
Video Game Marathon

Play two-player video games for an evening. If you don't have a gaming station, look into online games for two.

Date complete: _____

Favorite memories:

_____

_____

_____

_____

_____

Date Idea #19:
Lazy Living Room Picnic

🏠 🍴 🗣️ 🐾 💲

Set up a picnic layout on your living room floor. Order take-out and enjoy an easy and romantic dinner.

Date complete: _____

Favorite memories:

_____

_____

_____

_____

_____

Date Idea #20:
Bored? Try Board Games!

Enjoy an evening of playing your favorite board and card games. Maybe even try to make up your own.

Date complete: _____

Favorite memories:

_____

_____

_____

_____

_____

Connected
and Collected

Dates to get connected with
your city, or its culture and
community

Date Idea #21:
Pretend You're Tourists

Visit places in your city that tourists visit frequently. Spend your day doing touristy things, and take tons of photos!

Date complete: _____

Favorite memories:

_____

_____

_____

_____

_____

Date Idea #22:
Volunteer Together

Volunteer together at a local shelter or charity of your choosing. Talk about your experiences at the end of the day.

Place Photo Here

Date complete: _____

Favorite memories:

_____

_____

_____

_____

_____

Date Idea #23:
Donate Blood Together
✗ ❓

Do something meaningful together, and donate some blood.
Afterward, go get your sugar fill and replenish!

Place Photo Here

Date complete: _____

Favorite memories:

_____

_____

_____

_____

_____

Date Idea #24:
Attend a Live Play/Musical

Afterward, talk about your experience: What stood out to you? What were your favorite moments?

Place Photo Here

Date complete: _____

Favorite memories:

_____

_____

_____

_____

_____

Date Idea #25:
Visit a Farmer's Market

Visit a farmer's market and browse through all the vendors.
Purchase something unique for each other.

Place Photo Here

Date complete: _____

Favorite memories:

_____

_____

_____

_____

_____

Date Idea #26:
Visit a Museum

Visit a museum of your choosing. Afterward, talk about what you found interesting/boring.

Place Photo Here

Date complete: _____

Favorite memories:

_____

_____

_____

_____

_____

Date Idea #27:
Do a Corn Maze

Hold hands and try to find your way through a corn maze.
Take a photo when you finish to remember your victory!

Place Photo Here

Date complete: _____

Favorite memories:

_____

_____

_____

_____

_____

Date Idea #28:
Go Berry Picking

Go to a local farm and do some berry picking. Afterward, make something delicious with them.

Place Photo Here

Date complete: _____

Favorite memories:

_____

_____

_____

_____

_____

Date Idea #29:
Visit a Comedy Club

Watch some live stand-up comedy. Afterward, talk about your experience.

Place Photo Here

Date complete: _____

Favorite memories:

_____

_____

_____

_____

_____

Date Idea #30:
Go on a Ferry Ride

Enjoy a romantic ferry boat ride, and explore the area on the other side.

Place Photo Here

Date complete: _____

Favorite memories:

_____

_____

_____

_____

_____

Let'Get Creative!

Dates to get you thinking
outside the box and express
some creative energy!

Date Idea #31:
Make A Scrapbook

Gather some of your favorite pictures of the two of you,
and make your own keepsake scrapbook.

Place Photo Here

Date complete: _____

Favorite memories:

_____

_____

_____

_____

_____

Date Idea #32: Self Portraits

Paint or draw portraits of one another at the same time. Then, have a grand reveal!

Place Photo Here

Date complete: _____

Favorite memories:

_____

_____

_____

_____

_____

Date Idea #33:
Love Poems

Set a timer for 10 minutes at a time, and write the best love poem you can come up with. Share, and repeat.

Place Photo Here

Date complete: _____

Favorite memories:

_____

_____

_____

_____

_____

Date Idea #34:
Pumpkin Carving War

🏠 🎨 💲

Pick out two pumpkins, and see who can carve out the best design. Have a third party be the judge.

Date complete: _____

Favorite memories:

_____

_____

_____

_____

Date Idea #35:
Gingerbread House Wars

🏠 🍴 🎨 💲

See who can make the best gingerbread house. Have a third person be the judge. Then indulge in your creations!

Place Photo Here

Date complete: _____

Favorite memories:

_____

_____

_____

_____

_____

Date Idea #36:
Make a Time Capsule

Create a time capsule with a few pictures, keepsakes, etc...
Date it for a time in the future, and store it away.

Place Photo Here

Date complete: _____

Favorite memories:

_____

_____

_____

_____

_____

Date Idea #37:
Create A Short Movie

Start by planning the plot, then film your scenes, and use simple editing software to put it all together. Be fun and silly!

Place Photo Here

Date complete: _____

Favorite memories:

_____

_____

_____

_____

_____

Date Idea #38:
Create A Playlist

Put together a playlist of your all-time favorite songs. Save the playlist on both of your phones to play whenever.

Place Photo Here

Date complete: _____

Favorite memories:

_____

_____

_____

_____

_____

Date Idea #39:
Go People Watching

In an outdoor public area, point out a person in your sight, and together create an imaginary name and story for them.

Place Photo Here

Date complete: _____

Favorite memories:

_____

_____

_____

_____

_____

Date Idea #40:
Thrift Store Outfits

Visit a thrift store, and take turns choosing a complete outfit for the other person to purchase. Dress up, and take a photo!

Place Photo Here

Date complete: _____

Favorite memories:

_____

_____

_____

_____

_____

The Fun and The Furry

A mix of dates that involve furry friends and exciting adventures

Date Idea #41:
Play Mini Golf

Go to a mini-golf course, and play a couple of rounds of golf. Keep score to see who wins!

Place Photo Here

Date complete: _____

Favorite memories:

_____

_____

_____

_____

_____

Date Idea #42:
Visit an Arcade/ Rec Room

Visit a local arcade or rec. room and let your inner child out.
Let loose and just have some fun!

Date complete: _____

Favorite memories:

_____

_____

_____

_____

_____

Date Idea #43:
Visit an Aquarium

Learn about the different animals there. Take a picture with your favorite aquatic friend.

Date complete: _____

Favorite memories:

_____

_____

_____

_____

_____

Date Idea #44:
Visit a Zoo

Learn a new fact about an animal of your choosing. Take a picture with your favorite animal there.

Place Photo Here

Date complete: _____

Favorite memories:

_____

_____

_____

_____

_____

Date Idea #45:
Visit a Theme Park

Visit a theme park together, and if you can, challenge yourselves to go on a ride you haven't gone on before.

Place Photo Here

Date complete: _____

Favorite memories:

_____

_____

_____

_____

_____

Date Idea #46:
Visit a Haunted House

Around Halloween time, go visit a haunted house. Challenge yourselves to make it through (without wetting your pants!)

Place Photo Here

Date complete: _____

Favorite memories:

_____

_____

_____

_____

_____

Date Idea #47:
Play Some Billiards

Visit a billiards games room and learn how to play billiards: rules, techniques, and how to keep score. Then play a game!

Place Photo Here

Date complete: _____

Favorite memories:

_____

_____

_____

_____

_____

Date Idea #48:
Go Bowling

Visit a bowling alley, and play a couple of games together.
See how many strikes you can get!

Place Photo Here

Date complete: _____

Favorite memories:

_____

_____

_____

_____

_____

Date Idea #49:
Go to a Water Park

Go to a fun and exciting water park together, and
enjoy splish-splashing around in the sun.

Date complete: _____

Favorite memories:

_____
_____
_____
_____
_____

Date Idea #50:
Go Snow Tubing

Experience the child-like excitement of sliding down a hill in the snow with your partner by your side.

Place Photo Here

Date complete: _____

Favorite memories:

_____

_____

_____

_____

_____

Let's Get Learning!

Dates to get you outside of your comfort zone and learn something new

Date Idea #51:
What's This Plant?

Grab a plant-ID book, go for a nature walk,
and try to identify the plants that are local to your area.

Place Photo Here

Date complete: _____

Favorite memories:

_____

_____

_____

_____

_____

Date Idea #52:
Bird Watchers In Love

Grab a bird-ID book, go for a nature walk.
Try to identify the birds you see on your walk.

Place Photo Here

Date complete: _____

Favorite memories:

_____

_____

_____

_____

_____

Date Idea #53:
Couples Cooking Class

Take a couple's cooking class, and learn professional cooking techniques from a chef.

Place Photo Here

Date complete: _____

Favorite memories:

_____

_____

_____

_____

_____

Date Idea #54:
Couples Dancing Class

Take a couple's dancing lesson of a style of your choice, and learn some new moves to bring to the dance floor.

Place Photo Here

Date complete: _____

Favorite memories:

_____

_____

_____

_____

_____

Date Idea #55:
Pottery Making Class

Take a pottery-making class, and make something with
your own hands for each other.

Date complete: _____

Favorite memories:

_____

_____

_____

_____

_____

Date Idea #56:
Self Defence Class

Take a self-defense class either online or in person. Learn the important skill of how to protect yourself from an attacker.

Date complete: _____

Favorite memories:

_____

_____

_____

_____

_____

Date Idea #57:
Learn How to Make Ice Cream

🏠 🍴 🧠 💲

Find a recipe for homemade ice cream, grab your ingredients, and make a delicious bowl for the two of you to share.

Place Photo Here

Date complete: _____

Favorite memories:

_____

_____

_____

_____

_____

Date Idea #58:
Learn How to Make Bread

Find a recipe for homemade bread, grab your ingredients,
and make a delicious loaf for the two of you to share.

Date complete: _____

Favorite memories:

_____

_____

_____

_____

_____

Date Idea #59:
What's your love language?

Take online personality and love language tests to improve
your communication and understanding of one another

Place Photo Here

Date complete: _____

Favorite memories:

_____

_____

_____

_____

_____

Date Idea #60:
Learn Another Language

Challenge yourselves to learn a few basic phrases in another language.

Place Photo Here

Date complete: _____

Favorite memories:

_____
_____
_____
_____
_____

Actively Connected

Dates to boost your heart rate
and help you stay connected
through fun exercises.

Date Idea #61:
Go Ice Skating Together

Visit an ice rink and go ice skating together while holding hands. If one of you is a pro, have them blindfolded!

Place Photo Here

Date complete: _____

Favorite memories:

_____

_____

_____

_____

_____

Date Idea #62:
Challenging Hike

Challenge yourself to reach the top of the mountain. Take in the view together. Snap a pic to remember your victory!

Place Photo Here

Date complete: _____

Favorite memories:

_____

_____

_____

_____

_____

Date Idea #63:
Tandem Bike

Rent a tandem bike and learn how to ride it. Take turns being in the front seat, and try not to fall over!

Place Photo Here

Date complete: _____

Favorite memories:

_____

_____

_____

_____

_____

Date Idea #64:
Marco Polo- In The Water!

🏃 💲

Visit a swimming pool and play Marco-Polo in the water. It's more fun than you think!

Place Photo Here

Date complete: _____

Favorite memories:

_____
_____
_____
_____
_____

Date Idea #65:
Go Kayaking

Rent a two-person kayak and go for a boat ride. See how fast you can row through the water through good teamwork.

Place Photo Here

Date complete: _____

Favorite memories:

_____

_____

_____

_____

_____

Date Idea# 66:
Get Fit!

Browse online for a monthly exercise challenge, and try to stick to it for an entire month.

Date complete: _____

Favorite memories:

_____

_____

_____

_____

_____

Date Idea# 67:
Try Goat Yoga

Be nuzzled and nibbled by cute goats as you
are led through a relaxing yoga routine.

Place Photo Here

Date complete: _____

Favorite memories:

_____

_____

_____

_____

_____

Date Idea #68:
Roller Skating

Rent some roller skates (or use your own), and go roller skating at an indoor rink or somewhere outdoors.

Place Photo Here

Date complete: _____

Favorite memories:

_____

_____

_____

_____

_____

Date Idea #69:
Play Catch In The Park

Grab a frisbee or a soft ball, and go play catch at a nearby park.

Place Photo Here

Date complete: _____

Favorite memories:

_____

_____

_____

_____

_____

Date Idea #70:
Marathon or Charity Walk

Register and train for a marathon or charity walk together.
Take a photo at the finish line!

Place Photo Here

Date complete: _____

Favorite memories:

_____

_____

_____

_____

_____

Tasty Dates

Dates that involve exploring
your sense of taste and trying
new things

Date Idea #71:
Guess The Food!

🏠 ✗ 🍴 💲

Take turns being blindfolded while having the other partner
feed you different foods. Guess what you're eating!

Place Photo Here

Date complete: _____

Favorite memories:

_____

_____

_____

_____

_____

Date Idea #72:
Three Course Meal

Create a delicious three-course meal at home using
ingredients and flavors you've never experimented with.

Place Photo Here

Date complete: _____

Favorite memories:

_____

_____

_____

_____

_____

Date Idea #73:
What's In the Fridge?

🏠 ✕ 🍴

You're in a cooking show, and you're only given the items
currently in your fridge. Make something delicious!

Place Photo Here

Date complete: _____

Favorite memories:

_____

_____

_____

_____

_____

Date Idea #74:
Food Truck Festival

Visit a food truck festival. If your appetite allows it, get a little something from each food truck and then feast!

Place Photo Here

Date complete: _____

Favorite memories:

_____

_____

_____

_____

_____

Date Idea #75:
Go Wine/Beer Tasting
✗ $))

Go wine or beer tasting (whichever you prefer).
Purchase more of your favorite to take home.

Place Photo Here

Date complete: _____

Favorite memories:

_____

_____

_____

_____

_____

Date Idea #76:
Go Cheese Tasting

Visit a cheese factory and taste different types of cheese. Purchase more of your favorite to take home.

Place Photo Here

Date complete: _____

Favorite memories:

_____

_____

_____

_____

_____

Date Idea #77:
Go Chocolate Tasting

Visit a local store that allows you to sample different chocolates. Purchase more of your favorites to take home.

Place Photo Here

Date complete: _____

Favorite memories:

_____

_____

_____

_____

_____

Date Idea #78:
At Home Cooking Show

Set up a video camera. Pretend you're hosts on a cooking show, and teach the audience how to cook a meal. Be silly!

Place Photo Here

Date complete: _____

Favorite memories:

_____

_____

_____

_____

_____

Date Idea #79:
Explore a New Food

Eat at a restaurant that has a type of food that you've never had before.

Place Photo Here

Date complete: _____

Favorite memories:

_____

_____

_____

_____

_____

Date Idea #80:
Try a Food Box

✗ 💲

Order a food box online, and cook the recipe that comes
with it for a delicious and unique home-cooked meal.

Place Photo Here

Date complete: _____

Favorite memories:

_____

_____

_____

_____

_____

Double Dates

Fun dates to go on with
another couple to stay
socially connected

Date Idea #81:
Couples Scavenger Hunt

Come up with a scavenger hunt to send each other on as a couple. Meet up after and talk about your experience.

Date complete: _____

Favorite memories:

_____

_____

_____

_____

_____

Date Idea #82:
Do an Escape Room

Try to escape before the time runs out. Talk about your
experience afterward.

Place Photo Here

Date complete: _____

Favorite memories:

_____

_____

_____

_____

_____

Date Idea #83:
Couple's Getaway

Plan a couple's weekend getaway to a place all four want to go.

Place Photo Here

Date complete: _____

Favorite memories:

_____

_____

_____

_____

_____

Date Idea #84:
Couple's Cupcake Wars

Pick a theme, and have a cupcake war to see which couple can come up with the best-looking and tasting cupcake.

Place Photo Here

Date complete: _____

Favorite memories:

_____

_____

_____

_____

_____

Date Idea #85:
New Board Game Night

Play a board game that none of you have played before, and learn how to play it together.

Place Photo Here

Date complete: _____

Favorite memories:

_____

_____

_____

_____

_____

Date Idea #86:
Couple's Sleepover

Get together, watch movies, play games, stay up late, and have breakfast together the next morning.

Place Photo Here

Date complete: _____

Favorite memories:

_____

_____

_____

_____

_____

Date Idea #87:
Trivia Night

Attend a trivia night at a local pub or restaurant together,
and try to have your team win!

Place Photo Here

Date complete: _____

Favorite memories:

_____

_____

_____

_____

_____

Date Idea #88:
Host A Party Together

Host a fun-themed party together. Some examples of fun themes include wine tasting, murder mystery, etc...

Place Photo Here

Date complete: _____

Favorite memories:

_____

_____

_____

_____

_____

Date Idea #89:
Laser Tag

Grab another couple or two, go play some laser tag, and try to be the couple with the highest combined score.

Place Photo Here

Date complete: _____

Favorite memories:

_____

_____

_____

_____

_____

Date Idea #90:
Karaoke Lounge

Grab another couple and go to a karaoke lounge together.
Pick songs for each other to sing, and crush those notes!

Place Photo Here

Date complete: _____

Favorite memories:

_____

_____

_____

_____

_____

Save-Up Adventures

Bigger ticket item dates
to save up and plan for

Date Idea #91:
Smile, It's A Photoshoot!

Hire a professional photographer and get some romantic pictures taken someplace that is special to you.

Place Photo Here

Date complete: _____

Favorite memories:

_____

_____

_____

_____

_____

Date Idea #92:
Vacation time!

Take a vacation to a travel destination you've always
wanted to visit toegther. You deserve it!

Place Photo Here

Date complete: _____

Favorite memories:

_____

_____

_____

_____

_____

Date Idea #93:
Hot Air Balloon

Save up for a hot air balloon adventure.
Take a selfie with the fantastic view!

Place Photo Here

Date complete: _____

Favorite memories:

_____

_____

_____

_____

_____

Date Idea #94:
Go to a Sporting Event

Save up for good tickets to a sporting event or
game of your choice.

Place Photo Here

Date complete: _____

Favorite memories:

_____

_____

_____

_____

_____

Date Idea #95:
Date Cruise

Save up for an all-inclusive cruise adventure, and enjoy
a romantic sailing voyage.

Date complete: _____

Favorite memories:

_____

_____

_____

_____

_____

Date Idea #96:
Luxury Hotel for A Night

Rent a room at a luxury hotel in your city, and spend your entire day and night there. Room service and all!

Date complete: _____

Favorite memories:

_____

_____

_____

_____

_____

Date Idea #97: Music Concert

Save up for tickets to hear your favorite band/singer play live in a theatre.

Date complete: _____

Favorite memories:

_____

_____

_____

_____

_____

Date Idea #98:
Camping/Glamping

Drive to your dream camping location, and set up camp.
Consider renting an RV for a luxury camping experience.

Date complete: _____

Favorite memories:

_____

_____

_____

_____

_____

Date Idea #99:
Spontaneous Getaway

Plan a last-minute weekend getaway to someplace relaxing.
Leave all your stresses behind for a couple of days.

Place Photo Here

Date complete: _____

Favorite memories:

_____

_____

_____

_____

_____

Date Idea #100:
Disneyland/Disney World

What better place to visit together than the
happiest place on earth?

Place Photo Here

Date complete: _____

Favorite memories:

_____

_____

_____

_____

_____

Now It's
Your Turn

Blank templates to add
another 10 of your own date
ideas to your bucket list

Date Idea #101:

_____

_____

_____

Place Photo Here

Date complete: _____

Favorite memories:

_____

_____

_____

_____

_____

Date Idea #102:

_____

_____

_____

Place Photo Here

Date complete: _____

Favorite memories:

_____

_____

_____

_____

_____

Date Idea #103:

_____

_____

_____

Place Photo Here

Date complete: _____

Favorite memories:

_____

_____

_____

_____

_____

Date Idea #104:

_____

_____
_____

Place Photo Here

Date complete: _____

Favorite memories:

_____
_____
_____
_____
_____

Date Idea #105:

_____

_____

_____

Place Photo Here

Date complete: _____

Favorite memories:

_____

_____

_____

_____

_____

Date Idea #106:

_____

_____

_____

Place Photo Here

Date complete: _____

Favorite memories:

_____

_____

_____

_____

_____

Date Idea #107:

_____

_____

_____

Place Photo Here

Date complete: _____

Favorite memories:

_____

_____

_____

_____

_____

Date Idea #108:

_____

_____

_____

Place Photo Here

Date complete: _____

Favorite memories:

_____

_____

_____

_____

_____

Date Idea #109:

_____

_____
_____

Place Photo Here

Date complete: _____

Favorite memories:

_____
_____
_____
_____
_____

Date Idea #110:

_____

_____

_____

Place Photo Here

Date complete: _____

Favorite memories:

_____

_____

_____

_____

_____

Made in the USA
Las Vegas, NV
06 June 2022